Life Speaks . . .

What Is
It Saying
To You?

Life Speaks . . .
What Is
It Saying
To You?

Adrian R. Johnson

ARPress

ARPress

45 Dan Road Suite 5

Canton MA 02021

Hotline: 1(888) 821-0229
Fax: 1(508) 545-7580

Ordering Information:

Quantity sales. Special discounts are available on quantity purchases by corporations, associations, and others. For details, contact the publisher at the address above.

Printed in the United States of America.

ISBN-13:   Paperback   979-8-89356-643-7
             eBook   979-8-89356-645-1
             Hardback   979-8-89356-644-4

Library of Congress Control Number: 2024903489

COMMENTS

"Adrian Johnson's book Life Speaks . . . What is it saying to You? is a wonderful collection of poems that inspire, comfort and arouse the life-producing spirit in all of us. Each poem uniquely expresses the God-given qualities that are resident in this gifted author, father and soldier. Adrian's book is a breath of fresh air that will impart life into the souls of all its readers."

Sandy Mitchell IV, (Lifelong Friend)
Executive Pastor,
Church of the Harvest International

Adrian Johnson's book of poetry is spiritually stimulating! Reading these poems brings my imagination alive with wonder and refreshes my thirsty soul. I enjoy the sense of God's presence flowing forth from the carefully selected words. There is wisdom for life in the thoughts of the author, wisdom that is born of God. Contained in this book are words of meditation and inspiration to feed the souls of all who dare to open its cover. Grab a hot cup of tea and be prepared to dream dreams beyond your imagination and be blessed.

Wayne Garcia, US Army Chaplain.

"I was inspired by witnessing the depth and sense of humility Adrian displayed in his poems. It was obvious that he is truly a man after God and his spouse's heart. His words will also inspire others who seek to be pleasing to the Lord and the help-mates that the Lord has blessed them to have in their lives."

Dexter R. Freeman, DSW, LCSW
Director
Army-Fayetteville State University MSW Program
AMEDD Center & School
Fort Sam Houston, Texas

"My brother Adrian, a mighty man of God, has put on paper what has been placed on his heart. I'm sure these words will bless you as they have blessed me."

Michael Wenner
Former WCW professional wrestler and trainer
Member, Church of the Harvest International

Adrian Johnson's poetry was very inspiring to me. Each one that I read expresses his love to God, his wife and who Adrian is as a man in a very mixed up world of hate and despair. It seems to me that his poetry speaks volumes about love and how that intertwines with his love for God. I was deeply touched by his poem "This Is What You Mean To Me". I think about how much I love my own husband and want to speak the words in Adrian's poem to him.

Jody Garcia, Wife of a US Army Chaplain

Contents

SEASON 1 (SPRING)

Author's Prelude

Reflection: (S)piritual Poetry

The reflection during this season is on poems of a spiritual nature. Two terms come to mind regarding the spiritual; solemn and solace. The word solemn is described as sacred or formal. You will sense this as you read the poems covered throughout this representation of the spring season. Solace reflects comfort or consolation. These poems should be a source of refuge for you; a place for you to allow your mind to escape some of the harsh realities of life.

In this spiritual poetry, there is a peaceful and tranquil sentiment that transcends the natural realm. Reading these poems bears a refreshingly invigorating feeling. Place your mind at ease as you read this material. You should gain moments of peace as you reflect while reading. Likewise, ease of any tension is what you should receive. So, kick back, relax, and let yourself go as you read the poetry covered in this season of this book. I believe you will enjoy it.   Adrian

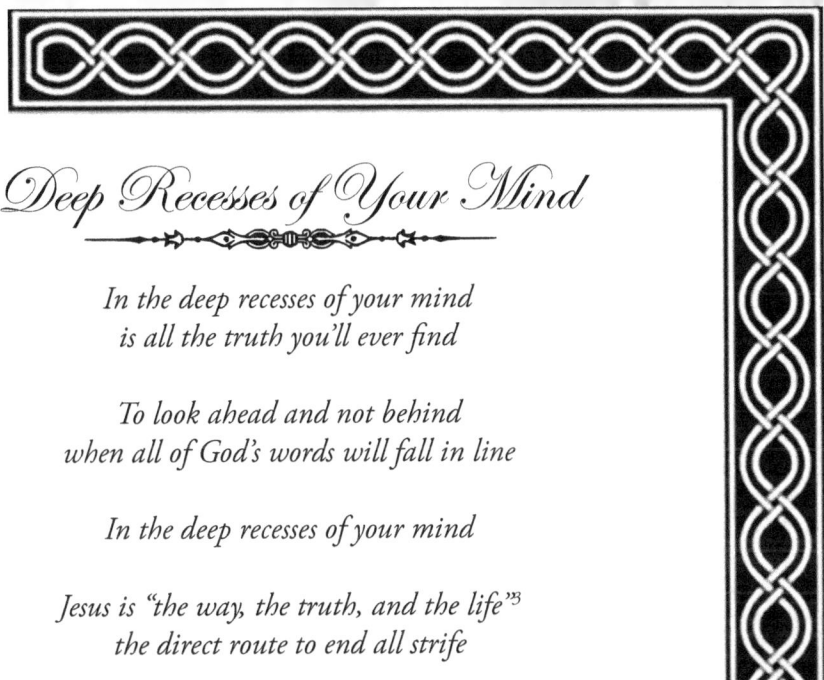

Deep Recesses of Your Mind

In the deep recesses of your mind
is all the truth you'll ever find

To look ahead and not behind
when all of God's words will fall in line

In the deep recesses of your mind

Jesus is "the way, the truth, and the life"[3]
the direct route to end all strife

The path that leads to eternal victory
just pray to Him and you will see

In the deep recesses of your mind

Continue to pray and the devil must flee
because of the price Jesus paid on the tree

Faith is what you hold on to when you feel you're going blind
as God's love for you lurks in the deep recesses of your mind

In the deep recesses of your mind

Written by:
A.R. Johnson

Who is This Man?

Who is this man, no ordinary man is He
for He makes even the demons tremble and flee

Who is this man, strong and mighty
walk around your wall seven times
and you too will have the victory

Who is this man, salient, radiant, possessor of the fire
ever ready and willing to take us all higher
"Hark the herald angels sing
Glory to the newborn King"[8]

Who is this man, no ordinary man could He be
for us He died on the cross, and rose on day three
He walked throughout the earth and Jesus is His name
about His Father's business He never besought fame

All authority and power have been given into His hand
cattle on a thousand hills, and in Him we possess the land
But I say again, who is this man
that all authority and power have been given into His hand

The Son of God, but no ordinary man is He
His name is Jesus and He is the King

Written by:
A.R. Johnson

4

Be Obedient to the Lord

To be obedient to the Lord
is the least of what I can afford
To be together and of one accord
the sentiment ornately stated all across the board

If your words ring loudly as they fill the sky
and your argument becomes dominant, are you better than I?
Nay I say, for the two shall become one flesh
when we put our thoughts together and do not settle for less

"Deep calleth unto deep,"[1] 'tis a communication for mankind
but how does it register when it enters the mind
Will we forever be lost, tossed by the waves of the sea
for a thought is an enigma, lost in the annals of eternity

Are we afraid to go deep because it will reveal just who we are?
it is through those shallow waters by which one will never go far

To escape the judgments of man is not truly a part of life
it compares to experiencing fullness, but never loving your wife

When faced with the depth of life's complexities
there is a voice that hovers across the seven seas
His message is clear, "sharper than any two-edged sword"[2]
our time is now, just be obedient to the Lord

Written by:
A.R. Johnson

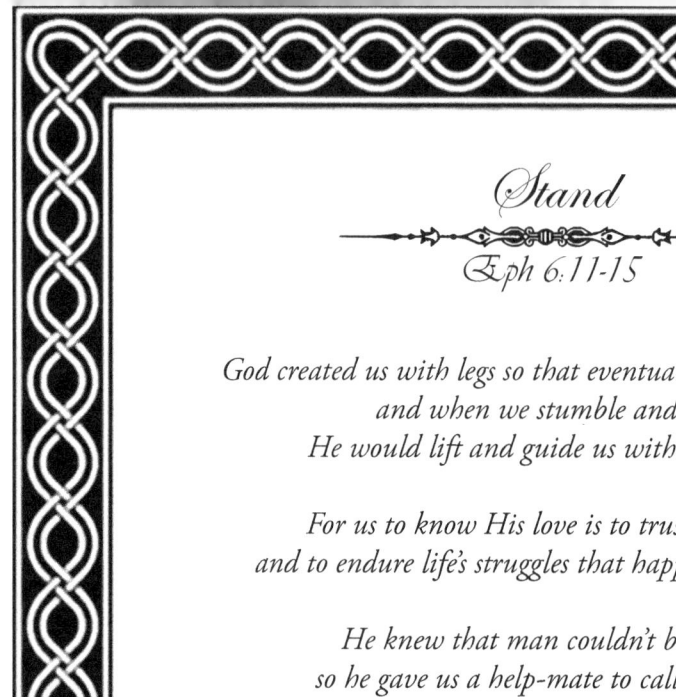

Stand

Eph 6:11-15

God created us with legs so that eventually we could stand
and when we stumble and fall
He would lift and guide us with His hand

For us to know His love is to trust His way
and to endure life's struggles that happen day-to-day

He knew that man couldn't be alone
so he gave us a help-mate to call our own
To be our guide when life we can't bear
pressing through each obstacle together
taking us from here to there

But exactly where is "from here to there?"

A woman wants a man who can consistently take the lead
but if he doesn't trust the Lord, how will he ever truly succeed

Now what about those who don't have legs or can't stand
in them God created a strong heart and will to move according to His plan

To stand is to remain fixated in one particular place
and to not move from there until God has imparted His grace
for if we move too soon from the throes of life
we preempt God's plan and invite pain and strife

Struggle and conflict should guide a couple toward deeper levels of intimacy
if they place their trust in Jesus, who died for you and me

When you feel as if you're in a whirlwind and there's no place for you to land
trust that God knows exactly where you are
and that all He wants is for you to
STAND

Written by:
A.R. Johnson

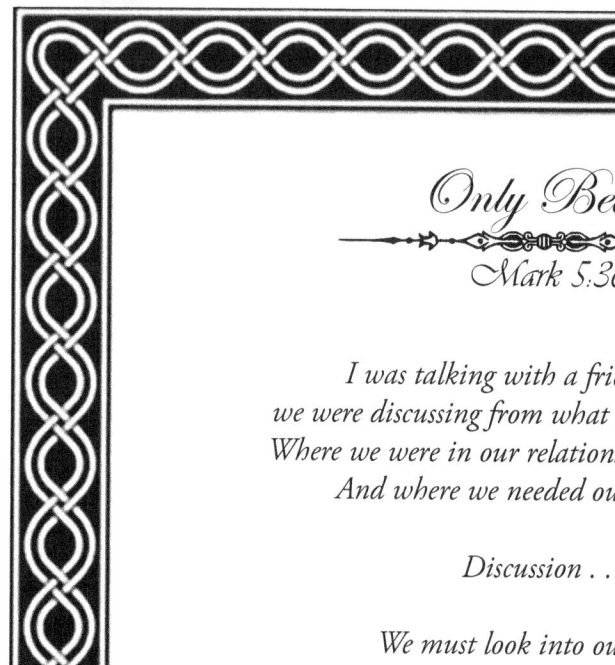

Only Believe
Mark 5:36

I was talking with a friend one day
we were discussing from what angle we could see
Where we were in our relationship with the Lord
And where we needed our focus to be

Discussion . . .

We must look into our world,
shape it the way we want it to be in Him
But if we want the greatest results in life
opportunity comes for doubt; but we must only believe

Trials make us hang our heads low;
we often wonder which way is up
If we're not careful we can be overcome by them
continue no longer in self-pity; for your victory only believe

Focus . . .

Jesus is the epitome of greatness
He heals all of our wounds and bruises;
even heals those of our family and friends, therefore . . .
from the spoken words of Jesus, "Do not be afraid; only believe"[4]

Conclusion . . .

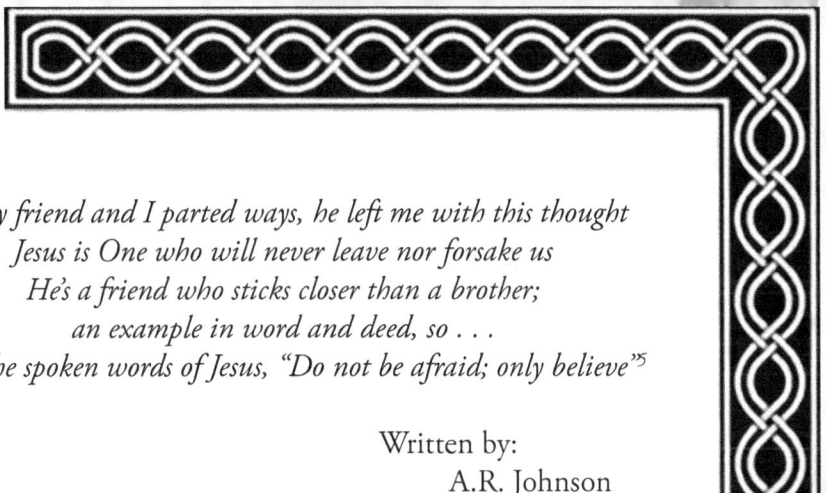

As my friend and I parted ways, he left me with this thought
Jesus is One who will never leave nor forsake us
He's a friend who sticks closer than a brother;
an example in word and deed, so . . .
from the spoken words of Jesus, "Do not be afraid; only believe"[5]

Written by:
A.R. Johnson

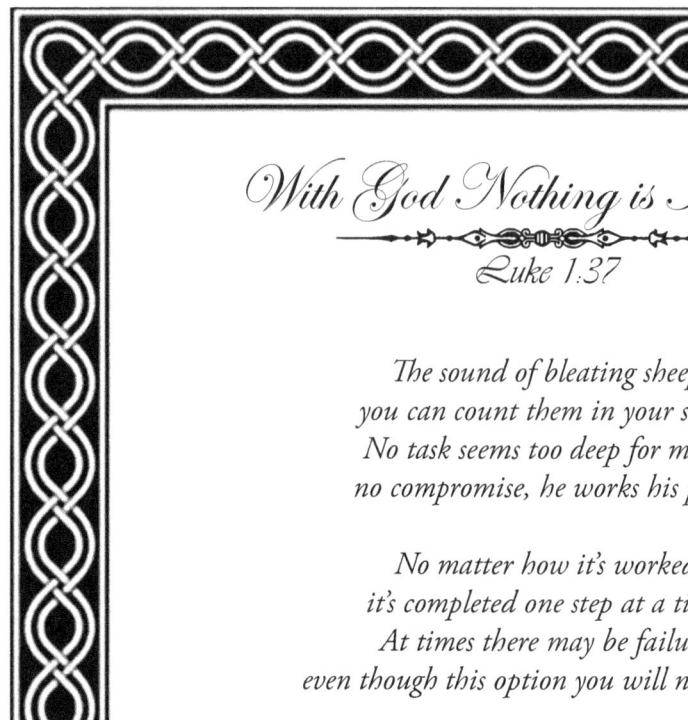

With God Nothing is Impossible
Luke 1:37

The sound of bleating sheep
you can count them in your sleep
No task seems too deep for man,
no compromise, he works his plan

No matter how it's worked
it's completed one step at a time
At times there may be failure
even though this option you will never find

in his mind he seeks answers to questions
answers for which the tallest tower he would climb
But no matter how far he would go
there is a limit to what he can know

In a man's life he will encounter a few obstacles
just let him live and not delay
"With God nothing is impossible"[6]
for His way is the only way

His thoughts are not our thoughts
because ours sometimes get us in trouble
When at the end of the day we collect our thoughts
we find that His thoughts were definitely more clever

He takes the simple things to confound the wise
and there's nothing new under the sun
When we come to realize that our possibilities end
"with God nothing is impossible"[7]—once again

Written by:
A.R. Johnson

10

The Servant

He kneels before the gate to pray
is hurried but won't be late today
Consecrates himself for a work to be done
bought with a price, he knows he's not his own

Dedicated beyond belief
a child at heart yet keeps the peace
Says "excuse me" rather than fills with pride
The Servant's life is the most denied

Where to go, what to do?
matters not to the servant because it's all about you
Travels about with his life on the line
no mission too great, no gesture too kind

To do for himself is not his will
he's quick to forgive and to please
And of all of life's great acclamations
the life of The Servant is the least of these

Written by:
A.R. Johnson

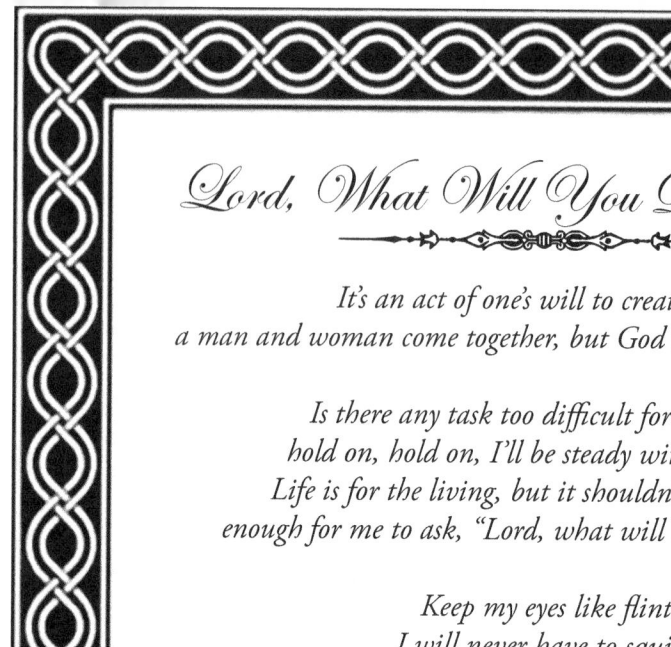

Lord, What Will You Do with Me?

It's an act of one's will to create a soul
a man and woman come together, but God must be the centerfold

Is there any task too difficult for the Lord?
hold on, hold on, I'll be steady with my sword
Life is for the living, but it shouldn't get too deep
enough for me to ask, "Lord, what will You do with me?"

Keep my eyes like flint
I will never have to squint
When I feel as though life is a disaster,
it is the Lord that I should seek after

There is no carbon copy or plan "B"
for the world God sent Jesus, and He died for you and me

So, when inside I feel empty and the road no longer, I see
I just stop and ask Him calmly, "Lord, what will You do with me?"

Written by:
A.R. Johnson

I Live for The Lord

Serve the Lord with gladness
I live for Him all the day long
Peace in my heart and unto mine
throughout all eternity

The oil flowing from Aaron's beard
flows down through my family tree
My wife and children are eternally blessed
I live for the Lord; therefore, I am set free

Come one, come all and hear the great news
you've lived to see another day
Blessed I count myself, for this I know
He dwells forever inside of me

Joy in my heart and love's pure light
develop each day in my soul
Another morning He has given me
My life, I live for the Lord

And when graciously everything starts to subside
I know this will not be the end
For in the life I've lived and given to the Lord
He will one day give back to me

Written by:
A.R. Johnson

His Grace

Break of dawn, morning comes
tis a new day, sing a new song
But how can I ever sing a new song?
my days are filled with trials and everything seems wrong

Troubling days, thundering skies
business lurks to circumnavigate our lives

People in and people out
movement is constant and all about
Olden day's men worked to take care of their families
Nowadays everyone works; who's taking care of our families?

No time to rest, no time to breathe
need to take a moment and put your mind at ease, but . . .
Life is too busy for me to believe
God's grace is sufficient for you and for me

Since when did the day's woes have to take a toll?
on your life each day as you watch it unfold
Get control, take a stand
place your life back in the Lord's hands

Every day has its trials, but you can get a new start
you have to slow your roll and think; make yourself smart

Everyday shouldn't be about turning a penny into a dollar
while chaos surrounds us and everything seems to scream and holler

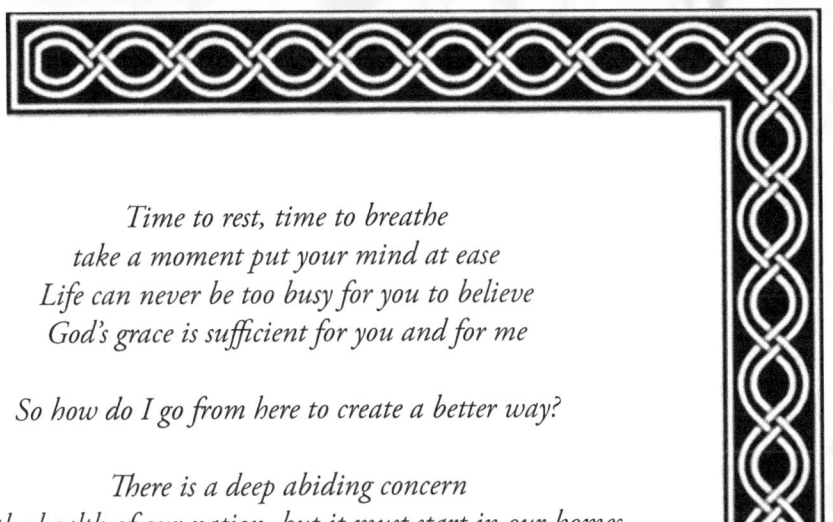

Time to rest, time to breathe
take a moment put your mind at ease
Life can never be too busy for you to believe
God's grace is sufficient for you and for me

So how do I go from here to create a better way?

There is a deep abiding concern
for the health of our nation, but it must start in our homes

Let's start spending more time with the ones that we love
instead of spending more dollars on our desires
as we feed and clothe

Our hearts and deeds must perpetually express what is right
as the impartation of God's grace aligns our sight

Weathering the vacillation of life's complexity
my life bears witness
HIS grace is sufficient for you and for me

Written by:
A.R. Johnson

SEASON 2 (SUMMER)

Author's Prelude

Reflection: (O)pen (Heart & Mind) Poetry

A flair for creativity is a necessary element for this season of the book. Surprise is a key factor in a suspense novel; however, with poetry the creative juices flow a little more smoothly when one has some idea of the topic of poetry to which one would be inclined. Intellectual acumen allows the mind to branch out a little further when reflecting on the poetry of this summer season.

Summertime brings refreshment and an opportunity for openness of mind. The warmth in the air relays a magnificent aura that will captivate the mind as this material is read. The flow is surreal; once started, it will be difficult to stop reading the poems introduced in this open venue. — Adrian

Character

There are going to be good days and bad days
but how we align ourselves to see

Becomes the determinant to our character development
and helps to preserve our dignity

Society exists all around us
our environment and surroundings we chose not

But our deeply hidden values
must be the thick of any plot

If the effort we give cannot direct or change
the life of one in need

We must examine the character we possess
for in this life, we lead

Every breath we take must contain the passion
and show that we're all called to plant a seed

Written by:
A.R. Johnson

Life is a Song

Peace and tranquility—beauty unforetold
yet mystery and chaos are what the mind seems to behold

A valley experience is profound;
a mountain inconsequential
And where do we find the answer
to why life is so irrational

Sometimes life deals blows that no one can counter
Are we part of the plight or are we part of the answer?
When situations become bitter, don't just swallow the pill
give it all you've got and conquer every hill

For life is too short to not capture the thrill

Distress comes to everyone, no need complaining just endure
Live to overcome; someone is always watching you
Life is a mystery soaring all night long
taking you through the clouds then bringing you back home

Birds sing melodies, whistling through the trees
capturing the moment as they pass through the breeze
Families come together, reuniting in summer fun
Today becomes tomorrow;
now you feel like life has begun

Make the transition from distressed to vibrant and strong
Life was abysmal for you, but now life is a song

Written by:
A.R. Johnson

The Heart

Beat… beat… life in the streets
Hard to keep up in the city heat
Boys draped with towels, girls cry foul
City officials oft laced with a scowl

Mothers pray for action
Fathers filled with passion

All of these are matters of The Heart

Created to sustain us, it cannot be denied
Broken inside of Him, the cause for which our Savior died
Down for a moment, but on day three He again would rise

The heart is resilient, always able to re-align

This – inside of fathers will return to their children
When we turn from our sin and our focus is to heal them
"Pride goes before destruction, a haughty spirit before a fall"

The heart is resilient, always able to resolve

All around us circumstances fail
Life pales, its impression scales
The wall, tells the tale, yet stands alone

All of these are matters of The Heart

Written by:
A.R. Johnson

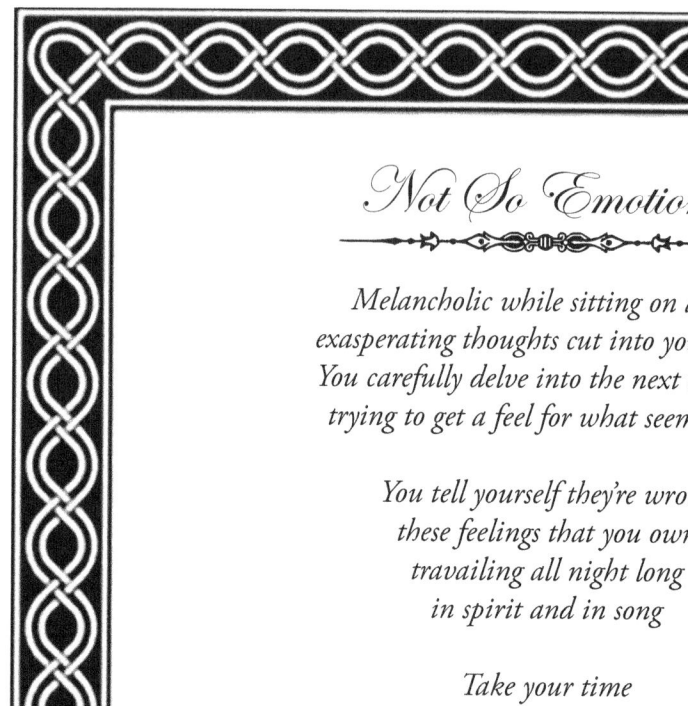

Not So Emotional

*Melancholic while sitting on a hill
exasperating thoughts cut into your mind
You carefully delve into the next moment
trying to get a feel for what seems right*

*You tell yourself they're wrong
these feelings that you own
travailing all night long
in spirit and in song*

*Take your time
joy is sublime
Awe-inspiring reflections
now capture your mind*

*When you can't steer your thoughts
from the lowly to the surreal
Prove to yourself that life isn't woeful
just be even-keeled and not so emotional*

Written by:
A.R. Johnson

I Believe

I look through the glass and what do I see
nothing that could possibly satisfy me
Is the glass half empty or is it half full?
Mentation shifts as I work through push and pull

Chronic dissonance stirs as my mind goes to and fro
remaining in upheaval, seems it's always on the go
What must I do as I need a reprieve?
Strengthen my resolve as I state what I believe

in my heart that contains both bad and good
but I have the ability to rule out the bad as I should

Relegate myself to see the beauty of life
eliminate the stress, reduce any form of strife
It's been often quoted the best things in life are free
make the change today—say to yourself "I believe"

Life is not easy; making sense of it is even harder
to let go and let God is to be a little smarter
Begin today as the stress of life you want to relieve
it starts with two words—say to yourself "I believe"

Having family without problems is hard to conceive
And that you actually have a role in it is something you will not receive
But if the other side of the rainbow you could ever perceive
May it one day become a reality as you say to yourself
"I believe"

Written by:
A.R. Johnson

21

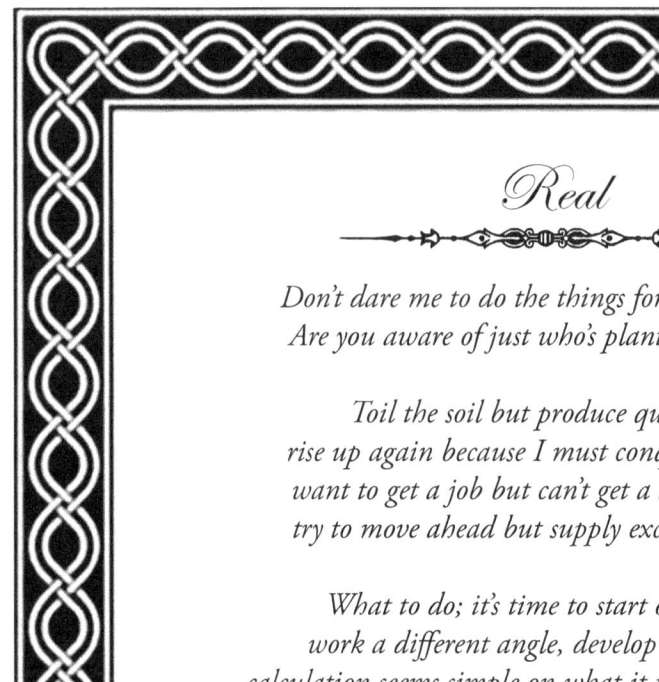

Real

Don't dare me to do the things for which I need
Are you aware of just who's planting this seed?

Toil the soil but produce quicksand
rise up again because I must conquer this land
want to get a job but can't get a helping hand
try to move ahead but supply exceeds demand

What to do; it's time to start over again
work a different angle, develop a new plan
calculation seems simple on what it takes to be a man
it's time to be real; the time is now to take a stand

Babes cry out, both hungry and tired
but what's a man to do when he just got fired
go out and get a job seems the answer to everything
whole lot of questions but what answers does society bring

Focal points change, getting older but not wiser
puts his money in the ground, feels the need to be a miser
tells his neighbor talk is cheap and that people don't know the deal
now is the time to take a stand and tell him it's time to be real

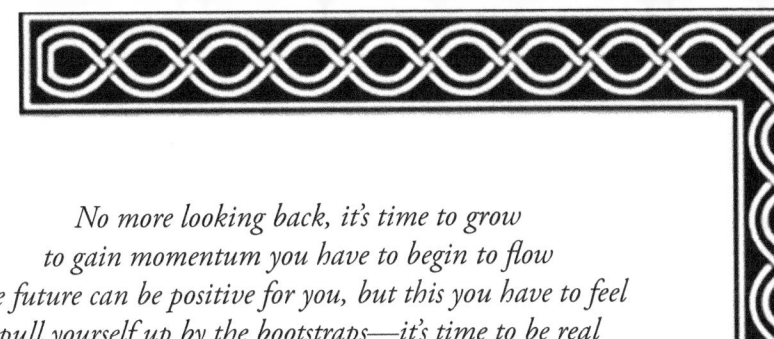

No more looking back, it's time to grow
to gain momentum you have to begin to flow
the future can be positive for you, but this you have to feel
pull yourself up by the bootstraps—it's time to be real

But on a serious note . . .

Yesterday is gone, today is a new day
change the way you think, change the words you say
start with a plan; something from which to build
it's time to take a stand—man—it's time to be real

Written by:
A.R. Johnson

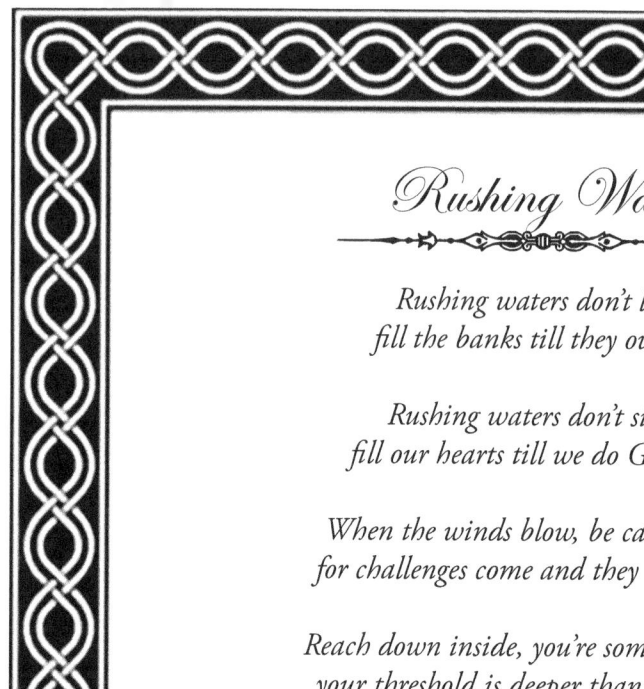

Rushing Waters

Rushing waters don't let go
fill the banks till they overflow

Rushing waters don't sit still
fill our hearts till we do God's will

When the winds blow, be calm, be still
for challenges come and they always will

Reach down inside, you're someone special;
your threshold is deeper than you believe
Clouds form to water the earth
and afterwards flowers bloom and trees grow leaves

Move ahead, don't lag behind,
for then your best you'll always find
will be before you when you tow the line
because perseverance carries us through time

When life's array seems a little slow
and the rainbow after the waters does not shine

Just look to the time those rushing waters return
and on your mountaintop proclaim that your day is fine

Written by:
A.R. Johnson

Changing Lives

Every good deed turned extends a hand to another
for no stone goes unturned
If you give, something will be given in return
you don't have to question it; your time will come

Everyone has a start date and at some time there will be an end
but the things that matter most are those that are done from within . . .
your heart

Plant a seed, but start today
for you will reap fruit along the way
It does not matter how great or how small
everyone with purpose will answer the call

Your life is a mirror and every day that you live
shows someone your example and shoes for them to fill
Are your shoes ones that someone would want to fill?

Everyone should ask themselves that question and not be afraid
for most have done wrongful things
for which they were forbade
Don't look back or think if I could start all over again
just act right now and produce a lifestyle change

All of us can do better; let no one deceive you
the life we live should be for others;
Mother Theresa and Dr. Martin Luther King Jr. knew
We were not created to act exactly the same way . . . but
we can get on the same sheet of music
and blend in perfect harmony

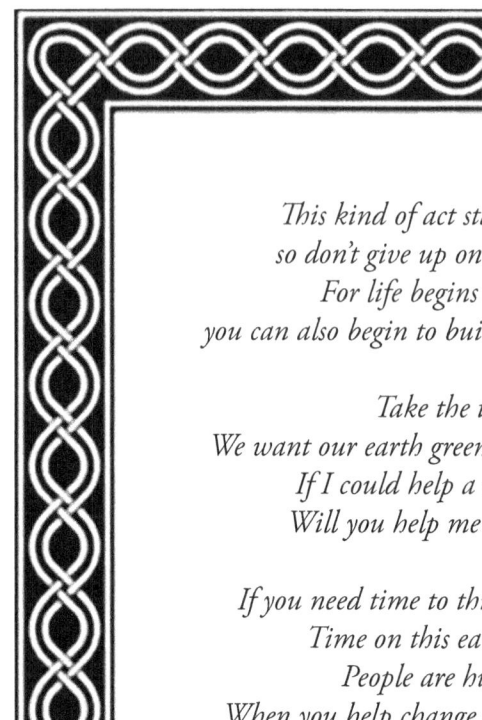

This kind of act starts with one person at a time
so don't give up on the action; fall right into line
For life begins to crash one day at a time
you can also begin to build, but your thoughts you must align

Take the time, please start now
We want our earth greener, but our character we must avow
If I could help a neighbor, I would do it now
Will you help me if I offered to show you how?

If you need time to think, then you need to think again
Time on this earth is not always our friend
People are hurting all over the world
When you help change the life of someone else, you help to
change your own

Written by:
A.R. Johnson

Put Your Hand in Mine

Dry the tears from your eyes
you don't have to cry anymore
What is it that you have fear of?
the element of the unknown compels you to drive on

Celebrate this day
live life one step at a time
Try not to count the mistakes you've made
I'll be there for you—put your hand in mine

Walk along the sea shore
feel the grains of sand on the bottom of your feet
Mount a horse and ride off in the distance
There's more to life than what you carry in your mind

Enjoy today; tomorrow is not promised
at the opportune moment the whole world could seem divine
Trials come however, to make us all stronger
all I want for you to do is put your hand in mine

The jungle is dense, yet the eagle soars high
animals scatter in search of their next meal
The rain pours and trees grow wide and tall
your mind tries to make sense of it all, but does it really matter?

Life consists of a series of events
which bind together to make the family element strong
When I think of the event that could remove the greatest amount of stress
That event would be for you to put your hand in mine

Written by:
A.R. Johnson

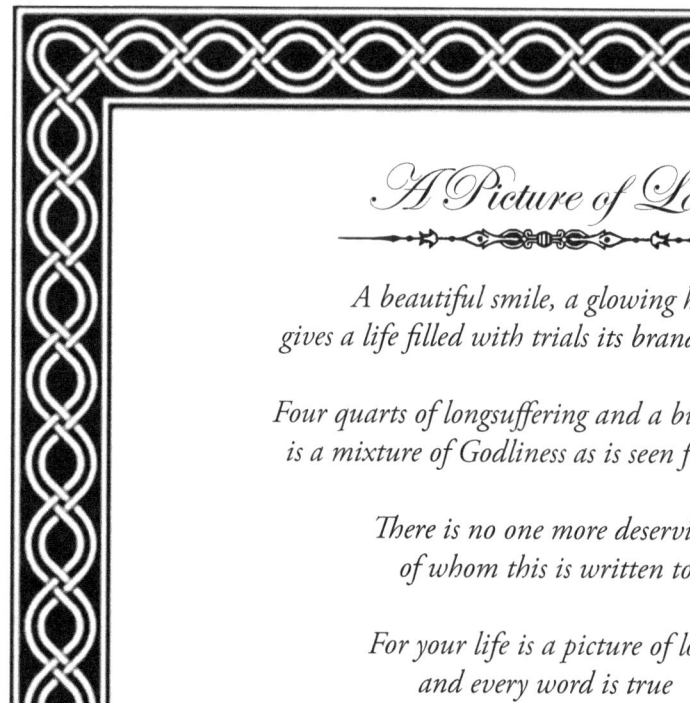

A Picture of Love

A beautiful smile, a glowing heart
gives a life filled with trials its brand-new start

Four quarts of longsuffering and a bushel of love
is a mixture of Godliness as is seen from above

There is no one more deserving
of whom this is written to

For your life is a picture of love
and every word is true

Let God's creation bear witness
coming from both near and far

Here stands a flower which blossoms all year around
and that flower is what you are

Written by:
A.R. Johnson

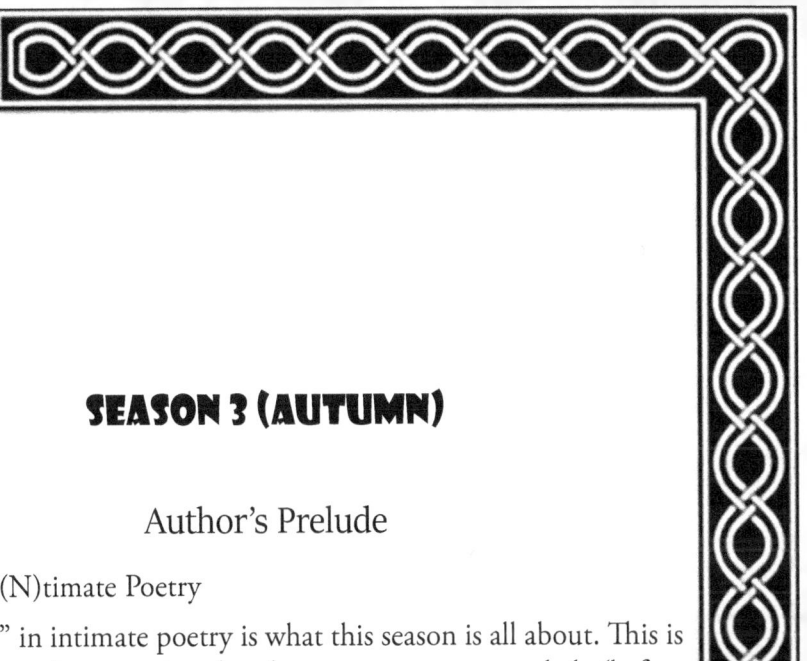

SEASON 3 (AUTUMN)

Author's Prelude

Reflection: I(N)timate Poetry

The "N" in intimate poetry is what this season is all about. This is the "in" thing—the attraction that draws a young man to a lady (before taking her as his wife). The warmth of summer is fading away. Cool briskness of autumn is headed their way. Heat generated from their passion begins to fill the air. Time is of the essence but there's no need to despair.

Nuptial comes to mind when reflecting on the "N" in intimate. In this intimacy is created the special bond that could be no greater defined than that which exists between a man and his wife. From the sleigh bells that ring in the winter through the church bells that ring after an autumn wedding, nuptials take place after a union between a man and woman becomes solidified by their strong and pervasive love for one another.

When reading the poems of this autumn season, one cannot help but become ingratiated with the sensations associated with newfound love. The words seem to leap off of the page as you become mesmerized by the content and where the text is taking you. This poetry should bring an excitement from which one can indulge. —Adrian

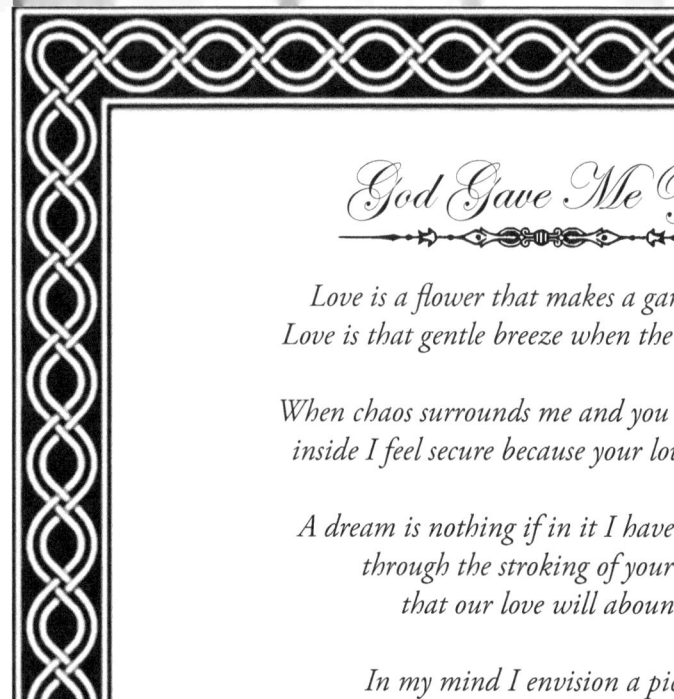

God Gave Me You

Love is a flower that makes a garden grow
Love is that gentle breeze when the winds blow

When chaos surrounds me and you are not near
inside I feel secure because your love is sincere

A dream is nothing if in it I have not found
through the stroking of your hair
that our love will abound

In my mind I envision a picture
of a sky that's forever blue

And God gave it all to me when He gave me you

Written by:
A.R. Johnson

You

What do I see when I look into your eyes?
not a reflection the sun casts, but a more pleasant surprise

Beauty overflowing yet gentle as a dove
what I see makes me realize I have found my true love

Intelligence, Sensitivity and Caring
are traits I see, to name a few

But when I look into your eyes
my heart skips a beat
because the reflection I see is of you

Written by:
A.R. Johnson

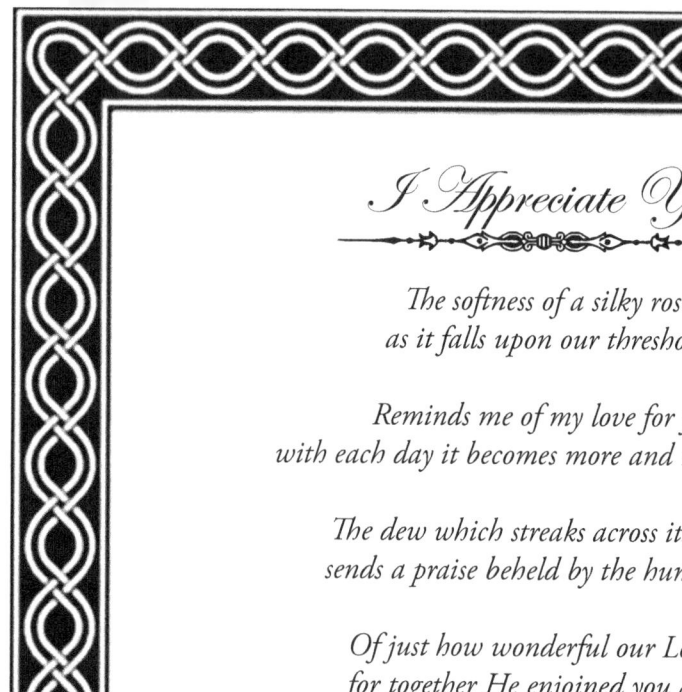

I Appreciate You

The softness of a silky rose
as it falls upon our threshold

Reminds me of my love for you
with each day it becomes more and more special

The dew which streaks across its petals
sends a praise beheld by the human eye

Of just how wonderful our Lord is
for together He enjoined you and I

Your birth - What a blessing to my life
it's a feeling I could never describe

All my world goes spinning round and round
when on our pillow my head I lie

But if all men should ever come together
and appreciate all the things their wives do

Every one of them would know in the way that I know
My life was not created to be lived without you

Written by:
A.R. Johnson

Gone With The Wind

Your beauty is so appealing

that it takes my breath away

Caught in the middle of nowhere

our lives have been swept away

A situation presents itself

as if seen on a movie screen

A haystack in a distant field

tree leaves blow pretty and green

And if on a windy summer day

thrust into the breeze our souls would mend

Nothing in life could be more beautiful with you

than the mystery that our lives have gone with the wind

Written by:
A.R. Johnson

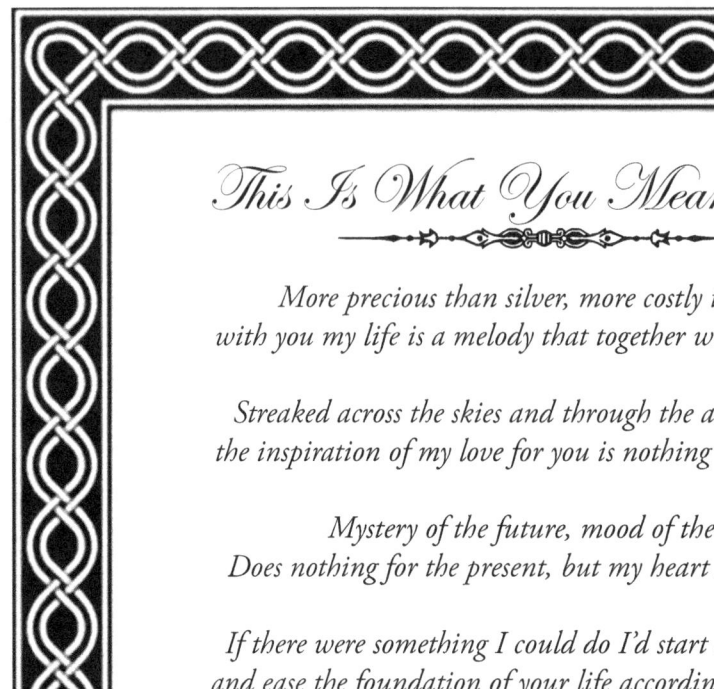

This Is What You Mean To Me

More precious than silver, more costly than gold
with you my life is a melody that together we watch unfold

Streaked across the skies and through the annals of time
the inspiration of my love for you is nothing short of divine

Mystery of the future, mood of the past
Does nothing for the present, but my heart still beats fast

If there were something I could do I'd start all over again
and ease the foundation of your life according to God's plan

For the precious Jewel given to me as a gift of the Lord
has sewn directly into my life the unity of one accord

No dream ever realized has removed the burden of complexity
As the life we share—my love—for this is what you mean to me

Written by:
A.R. Johnson

Be My Valentine

Love is a sentiment held very close inside
A very treasured moment you never want to hide

A flame that never dims, a light that always shines
It's something endemic, so be my valentine

My heart goes pitter-patter; I feel light on my feet
Feel I'm crusin' on autopilot and need to take a seat

But whether I am sitting still or I am on the grind
I need to know deep in my heart you'll be my valentine

Written by:
A.R. Johnson

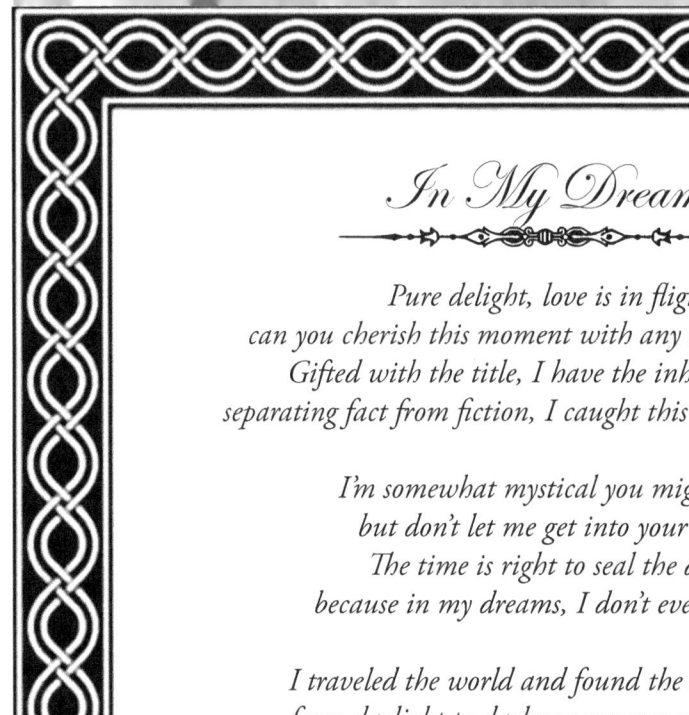

In My Dreams

*Pure delight, love is in flight
can you cherish this moment with any of your might?
Gifted with the title, I have the inherent right
separating fact from fiction, I caught this one at first sight*

*I'm somewhat mystical you might say
but don't let me get into your way
The time is right to seal the deal
because in my dreams, I don't ever sit still*

*I traveled the world and found the one for me
from daylight to darkness my eyes never failed
There have been hiccups in some areas of my life
but in this particular one, I have not been derailed*

*Simple as can be, the thoughts came together
functioning with purpose, there wasn't a storm I could not weather
Friction tried to align itself, but I said "Peace, be still"
for in my dreams the way develops to always carry me over the hill*

*Sights set ablaze, till the end of all days
nothing could go wrong, nothing missed in any phrase
I've discovered a way that sheds light and creates availability
for in my dreams my love and I share bliss with unwavering fidelity*

Written by:
A.R. Johnson

The Mystery of Love

Love is a mystery that is sweet and divine
Its essence is meticulously arrayed;
cannot be contained in a single package
Is as simplistic as white lilies blooming in an open field
The mystery of love

Savor its relevance
Its mood is symbolic yet unconventional
Its design cannot be encapsulated in our time;
is quaint but hard to define
The mystery of love

It's the blend of two souls becoming entangled,
through the annals of eternity, no way to be maligned
It's volcanic in nature; plunges deep into the abyss
is continued in the next chapter so you don't want to miss
The mystery of love

This mystery is reverential, but how does it occur
attempt to develop it into words, a description, or a gesture
Bears its own meaning, carries its own sound
cannot be defined in today's terminology and is aggravatingly profound
The mystery of love
… It's a mystery

Written by:
A.R. Johnson

Keep on Moving

Desperation is in the air
People feel it everywhere
To make the earth green you have to share
keep hope alive and don't despair

Join the fight; no time to keep still
pervade the atmosphere with a supernatural will
Inch by inch till you get your fill
just keep on moving, you'll develop your skill

What's your plight—defeat it with your might
not with talent and effort, but with a spirit that's contrite
Success is all around us; with your soul do it right
hearing the truth sometimes makes things a little tight

Where do you go to when you can't believe?
as the earth rotates, see the forest through the trees
Recognize the importance of life and offer a prayer from your knees
then keep on moving and let your body feel the breeze

Love the one you're with and keep your love alive
Endeavor to enjoy it; something for which you have to strive
Relationships require lots of hugs and making peace will keep the thrill
Keep on moving in a positive direction and nothing could seem more real

Written by:
A.R. Johnson

Where do we go to from here?

I placed my heart on the line
you took it and did not give it back
I saw it in your hands;
are you graceful or are you not?

I am dripping with sweat; poised for revenge
my fingers are calloused, mind eating away at me
This is just a dream, I convince myself
where do we go to from here?

You lead me down a valley
I follow you aimlessly;
take a moment to tighten my belt
I am going for the ride of my life

Wait just a moment—things are beginning to shift
if I ignore you just a little, then you start to hiss

You hear the development of laughter in the cool breeze
"Where do we go to from here?" You ask, as you fall to your knees

With my head held back and my hands to my face
I realize at this point there will be another day
Map out our future and have no fear,
As I ask myself, "Where do we go to from here?"

Life is filled with days for which you go without sleep
And you try to play catch-up before you get in too deep
But when playing cat and mouse with love bells in the air,
Sit back and ask yourself, "Where do we go to from here?"

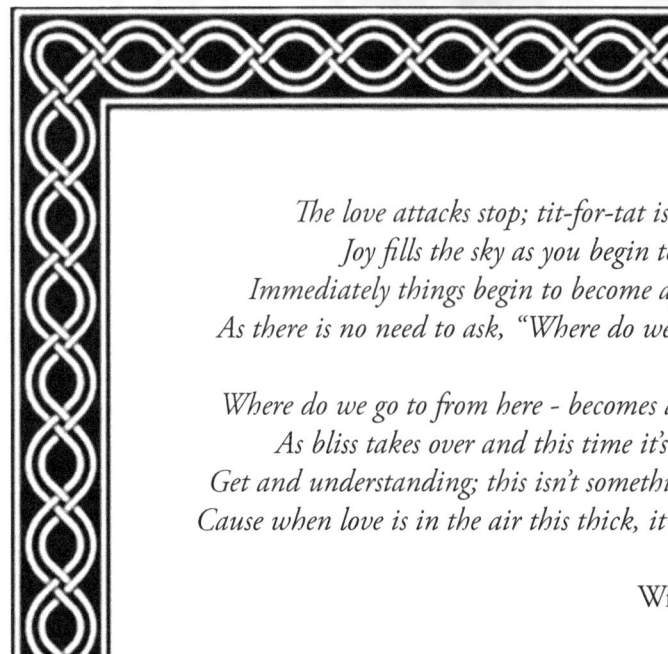

The love attacks stop; tit-for-tat is on the low
Joy fills the sky as you begin to let go
Immediately things begin to become apparently clear
As there is no need to ask, "Where do we go to from here?"

Where do we go to from here - becomes a thing of the past
As bliss takes over and this time it's going to last
Get and understanding; this isn't something you need to feel
Cause when love is in the air this thick, it is absolutely surreal

Written by:
A.R. Johnson

SEASSON 4 (WINTER)

Author's Prelude

Reflection: (G)roup (Family) Poetry

Picture this—being encamped round about a sparkling fireplace with your group or family, roasting marshmallows and singing lullabies. In the cold of winter, the family or group element is the strongest bond that can be formed to fit this particular occasion. Winter sometimes brings extremely cold temperatures, but the love found in groups (families, friends, and associations) trumps that brought on by weather patterns.

To maximize the effectiveness of this season, the warmth created from these poems is buttressed by their realism. During the winter season, experience coming together as a group or a whole. Sense yourselves pulling together to wrap up the old year and to start the new year afresh. Lastly, regarding the dynamic attained by these poems of several individuals comprising a group, resolve in your mind to do better in your group in the coming year and close out your winter strong. — Adrian

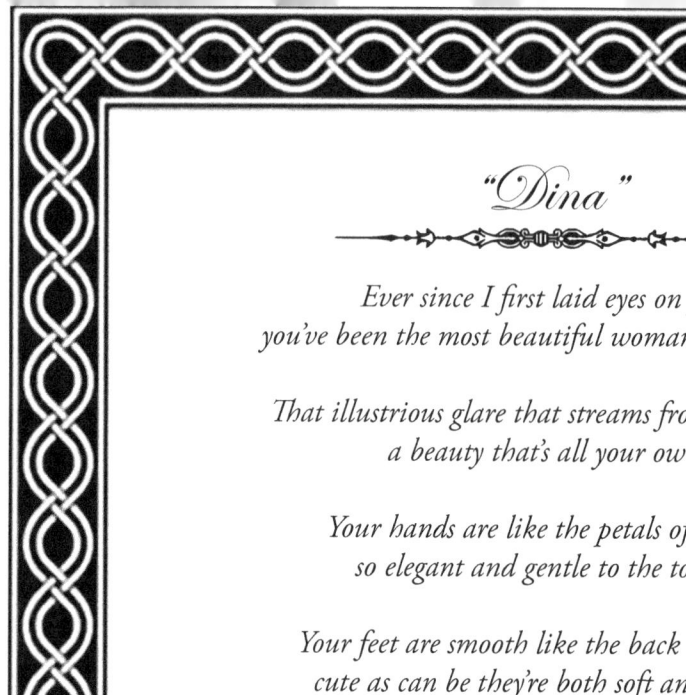

"Dina"

Ever since I first laid eyes on you
you've been the most beautiful woman I've known

That illustrious glare that streams from your eyes
a beauty that's all your own

Your hands are like the petals of a rose
so elegant and gentle to the touch

Your feet are smooth like the back of a dove
cute as can be they're both soft and plush

The character you possess is strong
the very depth of your mind is sound

Every time I kiss you it tastes like wine
each time you smile it's absolutely profound

My God, how I admire your gorgeous eyes
and the fullness of your hair is so fine

But the one thing I love about you the most
is the fact that you will always be mine

Written by:
A.R. Johnson

Isaiah ~ Warrior at the Heart

When you were a boy, a racecar you wanted to drive
and for the vision before you, anyone would have complied
So full of life, vibrant but care free
a force to be reckoned with you wanted to be

Steely-eyed but suspicious with an insatiable desire to run
reach for the sky and capture the sun
At a moment's notice your life had begun
laser focused to blaze a trail, even if it were just for fun

Never gave us a dull moment . . . you set our spirits free
from toddler to adolescent, you displayed a certain destiny
wrapped in cartoons and comics and maintaining anonymity
a warrior at the heart, you could be what you wanted to be

Fade to adulthood . . .

Set the stage, prepare the way
your victory is at hand
Clear the path and announce on high
this warrior at the heart comes to possess the land

Written by:
A.R. Johnson

Mark – Strong-Willed and Fearless

From a boy to a man, you grew up fast

From pushing battery-operated train sets
to pulling at the hearts of people
You had a determination that persisted
beyond the natural realm

An audacious child not knowing his next step or meal
but musters enough courage to picture the next day
And if he could just get there
one step at a time

Eventually his will produces vision for a lifetime

But life is not over, so to where from here
Put your trust in the Lord and do not fear

Written by:
A.R. Johnson

44

Nicole–My Little Lamb

Jesus is the Lamb that was slain for the sins of the world,
and you are my little lamb—secure in my world

I named you from your mother's womb
you had an immediate effect on my life
I felt all my burdens were lifted
you removed any element of strife

Your preteen years were a joy to me
like spoiling your mother's surprise birthday party
From always needing your underwear to match your clothes
to doing your plie and bouncing on your toes

Stroke of genius, touch of brawn
Feathered like a paintbrush but delicate like a pawn

Onward and upward you're now a Soldier
and as you grow finer, you'll become even bolder
to raise a generation with a lifelong plan
From a baby to a Soldier
Nicole you'll always be my little lamb

Written by:
A.R. Johnson

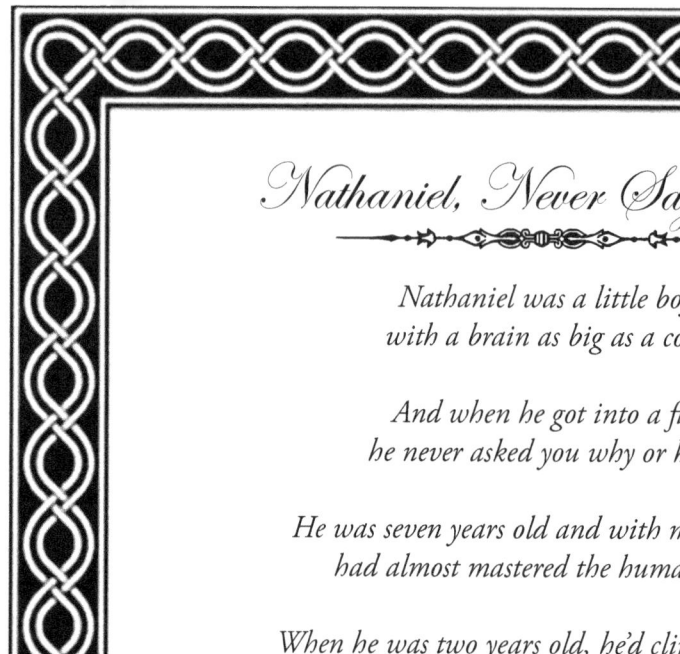

Nathaniel, Never Say Never

Nathaniel was a little boy
with a brain as big as a cow

And when he got into a fix
he never asked you why or how

He was seven years old and with much grace
had almost mastered the human race

When he was two years old, he'd climb any tree
and at age five, cried after being stung by a bee

He was so smart that he could receive
a double-promotion

Yet he belly-ached, whined,
and even caused commotion

But when all was said and done
and the hummingbird was singing

If he couldn't play outside
he was never allowed to do anything

Written by:
A.R. Johnson

Elijah – Man of Fire

Full of vigor, born for esteem
Not a statuesque young man, but powerful before the Lord
Calmness abounds you, humility builds your might
your words are few, but have the strength to draw a sword

Humble in spirit, grand in deed
focused on high, prayer always at your side
Able to carry on continually the mission before you,
God forever remains your guarantee

Elijah—you are man and spirit
draw your might from your spirit
Recognize your inner being
then your true character will shine freely

Can you account for every minute?
give your whole day to the Lord

Only He can fully sustain you
focusing on your every need

My prayer is that your life
every day God will guide
For every tear that I had cried
brought Jesus closely to your side

Life is not over; it is only just beginning
have no fear there is work to be done
Conquest came in the days of the prophet . . .
Elijah—Man of Fire
grab your sword for there's a fight to be won

Written by:
A.R. Johnson

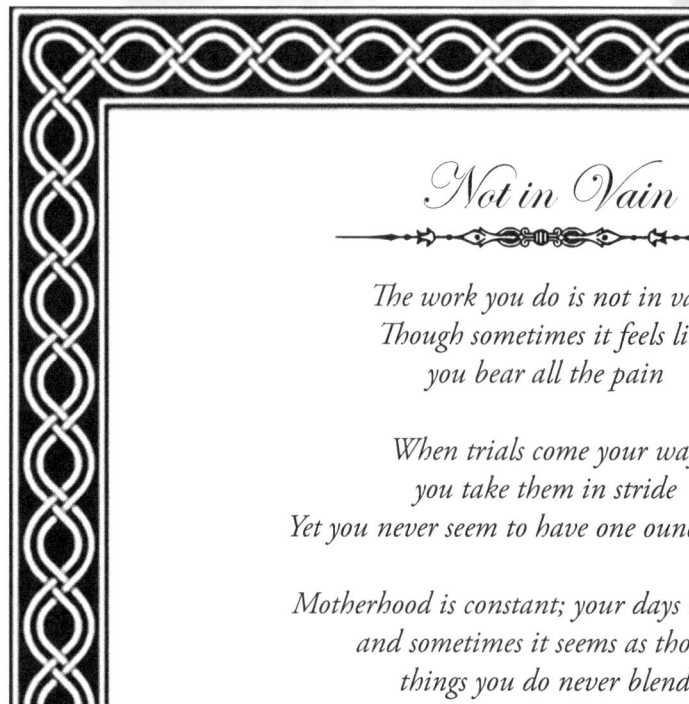

Not in Vain

The work you do is not in vain
Though sometimes it feels like
you bear all the pain

When trials come your way
you take them in stride
Yet you never seem to have one ounce of pride

Motherhood is constant; your days never end
and sometimes it seems as though
things you do never blend

But when the day is all over
and everything is said and done

Just know from the bottom of my heart
that you are my number one

Written by:
A.R. Johnson

The Life of a Soldier

The life of a Soldier is viewed through his walk
his body is erect
each step is perfectly ordered
one foot placed directly in front of the other

He forever looks forward
from his hair down to his shoes
he is poignantly sculptured
he is the embodiment of the professional Soldier

He must be serene
must always look ahead
for each day presents new challenges
and the life of a Soldier must continue to go on.

Written by:
2LT A.R. Johnson

Called to Duty

Fix bayonets, prepare to enter the fight
Surprise attack awaits over the hill

Perdition lurks for those not skilled
Retreat is for the faint, build up your might

Tomorrow is not promised, today is at stake
Our neighbors produce on every side

Teamwork is the endeavor our hearts seek after
Duty is never limited; it's a call that you make

Introspection is key, relevance a factor
What's your plot if your future you will not seek after?

This noble deed is a call for all mankind
Stand up and strong and make up your mind

In the end what do you have if a story it does not tell?
For common man endures fright and his own private hell

When you dawn the uniform for the very last time
Having answered the call of duty for God and for man

Your understanding will now be enlightened
For you truly answered the noblest deed of mankind

Written by:
A.R. Johnson

Come Together

A single unit marches in stride
not always synchronized but follows a plan
Their leader develops with the help of the group
the mindset is strong; the group is at its peak

Devastation occurs—does the group fall apart?
one says, now is not the time to conquer the hill
Regroup at once! What is the game plan?
to come together is an act of will

If not today, then when will the day come?
gather all of your friends
Make a declaration before the council
no moment will ever seem quite like the present

Aspiration piles high
demolition draws nigh
A dilemma unfolds
Come together—finish the fight

Morality is on edge
what is the right decision to make?
The answer lies before you
come together and complete your objective

Written by:
A.R. Johnson

LIFE SPEAKS...WHAT IS IT SAYING TO YOU?

Works Cited

The Holy Bible, Authorized King James Version. Ultra Thin Reference Edition. Cornerstone Bible Publishers. Nashville, TN: Cornerstone, 1991 (Psa 42:7)

The Holy Bible, Authorized King James Version. Ultra Thin Ref Ed. Cornerstone Bible Publishers. Nashville, TN: Cornerstone, 1991 (Heb 4:12)

The Spirit-Filled Life Bible New King James Version. Jack W. Hayford. Gen. Ed. Nashville, TN: Thomas Nelson Publishers, 1991 (Jn 14:6)

The Spirit-Filled Life Bible New King James Version. Jack W. Hayford. Gen. Ed. Nashville, TN: Thomas Nelson Publishers, 1991 (Mar 5:36)

Ibid., 4.

The Spirit-Filled Life Bible New King James Version. Jack W. Hayford. Gen. Ed. Nashville, TN: Thomas Nelson Publishers, 1991 (Luke 1:37)

Ibid., 6.

Mendelssohn, Felix. "Hark the Herald Angels Sing." The Cambridge Hymnal. Cambridge University Press, 1967.

The Spirit-Filled Life Bible New King James Version. Jack W. Hayford. Gen. Ed. Nashville, TN: Thomas Nelson Publishers, 1991 (Prov 16:18)

www.ingramcontent.com/pod-product-compliance
Lightning Source LLC
Chambersburg PA
CBHW060354130626
46553CB00003B/1231